Chickens on a Farm

Abbie Mercer

PowerKiDS press™

New York

Published in 2010 by The Rosen Publishing Group, Inc.
29 East 21st Street, New York, NY 10010

First Edition

Editor: Amelie von Zumbusch
Book Design: Kate Laczynski
Photo Researcher: Jessica Gerweck

Photo Credits: Cover, pp. 1, 5, 7, 9, 13, 15, 19, 21, 23, 24 Shutterstock.com; p. 11 © David Aubery/Getty Images; p. 17 Peter Anderson/Getty Images.

Library of Congress Cataloging-in-Publication Data

Mercer, Abbie.
  Chickens on a farm / Abbie Mercer. — 1st ed.
      p. cm. — (Barnyard animals)
  Includes index.
  ISBN 978-1-4358-3840-6 (library binding) — ISBN 978-1-4042-8063-2 (pbk.) —
ISBN 978-1-4042-8064-9 (6-pack)
  1. Chickens—Juvenile literature. I. Title. II. Series.
  SF487.5.M47 2010
  636.5—dc22
                                    2008049058

Manufactured in the United States of America

Contents

Chickens live on farms. Chickens are birds, but most chickens cannot fly.

As all birds do, chickens have **beaks**. Unlike most birds, adult chickens have red **combs**.

Chickens that live on small farms live in chicken houses, called **coops**.

On bigger farms, chickens live in big barns.

Chickens eat mostly grains, such as seeds. Chickens also **scratch** the ground to find bugs to eat.

Male chickens are known as roosters. Roosters say, "Cock-a-doodle-do."

Female chickens are called hens. Hens lay eggs. Hens warm their eggs by sitting on them.

People gather some eggs to eat.
Fried eggs, cakes, and French
toast are made with eggs.

Baby chickens break out of other chicken eggs. Baby chickens are called chicks.

Chicks are soft and fluffy. Have you ever held a chick?

Words to Know

beak

comb

coop

scratch

Index

Web Sites

Due to the changing nature of Internet links, PowerKids Press has developed an online list of Web sites related to the subject of this book. This site is updated regularly. Please use this link to access the list:
www.powerkidslinks.com/byard/chickens/